# Demonstrations
# II: On Love
# VII: On Penitents

*Aphrahat*

Copyright © 2015 Beloved Publishing

All rights reserved. No part of this book may be reproduced, scanned, or distributed in any printed or electronic form without permission.

Printed in the United States of America

ISBN:1631741098

## Demonstration II: On Love

**1.** Surely, beloved, all the law and the prophets depend upon the two commandments, as our Saviour said: "The law and the prophets are too little to convince him who will not be persuaded." Therefore our Saviour said: "On these two commandments hang the law and the prophets," that is: "A man shall love the Lord His God with all his soul, and with all his might, and with all his substance"; and that a man also "shall love his neighbor as himself."

**2.** And when thou proceedest to the examination of these two commandments, upon the power of which depends all the law and the prophets, thou mayest perceive if these two commandments, on which depends all the power of the law and the prophets, are received in the hearts and in the minds of men, or if the law and the prophets which have been written, have not been sought, as it is written that "for the just the law is not appointed, but for the evil doers." On account of the wicked, therefore, the law has been appointed. And if righteousness had remained among men law would not have been needed. Again, if a law had not been appointed, the power of God would not have been known in all our generations, and in all the miracles which He showed. By the transgression of the commandment of the house of Adam death was decreed against the world, and the power of God manifested when all men arise at the end which removes the rule of death. On account of the sinners which were in the days of Noah the power of God was manifested in the waters of the flood. And Abraham, because he observed the righteousness which is in the law before the law was appointed, had manifested in him the power of God by means of righteousness, when he brought back the spoil of Sodom by the power of his God and did not put forth his hand upon the booty; and |19 God said to him after that day: "Thy reward is multiplied by thy righteousness." And he upon whom the law had not been imposed manifested the works of the law, which the law of his righteousness did not require. Thus also in the case of Isaac and Jacob his sons, there was no necessity for them (to obey the law), because the law had not yet been imposed for their righteousness, for their father commanded them to act worthily and justly; as it is written that the Lord said concerning Abraham: "I know him, that he will command all his sons after him that they keep all My commandments." Also Joseph kept the righteousness which is in the law when he was not obedient to his mistress. For he said: "How shall I do this great wickedness and sin against God?" And Moses also, for he observed the righteousness which is in the law when he denied that he should be called a son to the daughter of Pharoah; on account of this the Lord made him worthy that through him He gave the law to His people. For all these manifested the works of the law, also for their righteousness the law had not been imposed and they were a law unto themselves.

**3.** When the time of the law was at hand it was added on account of transgression. And He showed that it was an addition. And wherefore, then, was this addition? except on account of the calling of the Gentiles which was foretold before the law was promised. And that law was the keeper and teacher until that Seed should come in whom the Gentiles were blessed. For the word of the oath which was promised to Abraham is also a covenant of the promise; God said unto him, "In thy seed shall all the Gentiles be blessed." And this word, which is a covenant, placed four hundred and thirty years before the law, was a promise to Abraham that the Gentiles in his seed, which is Christ, should be blessed. And the law was four hundred and thirty years after these things. For when Abraham received this promise he was eighty-five years old, and from that time until Jacob went to Egypt was two hundred and five years, and from the time that Jacob went to Egypt and until the people came forth by the hand of Moses was two hundred and twenty-five years.

**4.** And the cause of their sojourning is designated, for the children of Israel abode four hundred and thirty years in the land of Egypt. And wherefore, beloved, when they dwelt there two hundred and twenty-five years was four hundred and thirty years written for |20 them? if not on account of that hour of which God said to Abraham: "Know of a surety that thy seed shall be a sojourner in a land which is not theirs, and they shall serve among them, and they shall bring them into bondage four hundred years. For at that time in which this word was spoken to Abraham, there shall be unto thee an offspring, by faith it was formed in the heart of Abraham, as it is written: "Abraham believed in God, and it was reckoned unto him for righteousness." And also the word concerning the servitude which his sons should serve in Egypt was conceived in the heart of Abraham, and he began to be anxious as to how his seed should be in servitude, and his heart was serving in Egypt. Likewise also Isaac and Jacob were taking thought about the servitude, and they were in thought serving in the midst of Egypt. And the bondage was promised concerning the seed of Abraham before they were born; for the word was fifteen years before the birth of Isaac, and the promise of the bondage was two hundred and five years before their entering Egypt, and the promise that in the seed of Abraham all peoples should be blessed was four hundred and thirty years before the law. And the law was not able to make void the promise, henceforth the law was an addition with regard to this word of promise until the time should come.

**5.** And that word was preserved one thousand seven hundred and ninety-four years from the time it was promised to Abraham until the Advent, and that word was in observation one thousand three hundred and sixty-four years after the imposition of the law. And the word was four hundred and thirty years older than the law, and when it came it made ineffectual observances of the law. And the law and the prophets are included in these two commandments or which our Lord spoke, for the word is written: "All the law and the prophets prophesied until John the Baptist." And our Lord said: "I have not come to destroy the law and the prophets, but to fulfil them." Again it is written: "The truth of the law is through Jesus."

**6.** And how, then, were the law and the prophets lacking, when it was necessary that they should be fulfilled? if not because the testament was hidden in them which is itself the word of promise. For that testament which was given to Moses was not sealed until this last testament should come, which is also the first, because it was promised, it was signed by the death of Him who was to come of the testament, and the two testaments were confirmed (N.B. this |21 whole passage is obscure and the translation, following the Latin rather closely, little more than a guess): "And He made them both one, and the law of the commandments He abolished by His precepts." For the uses of the law are abolished by the advent of our Life-giver, and He offered up Himself in the place of the sacrifices which are in the law, and He was led as a lamb to the slaughter in the place of the lambs of propitiation, and He was killed for us (as) a fattened bull, that there might be no necessity for us to offer the offspring of cattle. He came and He was lifted up upon the cross; oblations and sacrifices are not required from us; He gave His blood in place of all men, that the blood of animals might not be required of us; He entered the sanctuary which was not made by hands, and He became the priest and minister of the holy place. For from the time in which He came He abolished the observances which are of the law, and from the time that they bound Him the festivals were bound for them by chains; and because they wished to judge the innocent One He took the judges away from them; and because they rejected His kingdom He took away the kingdom from them, for He came whose the kingdom is; and He ascended a living sacrifice in our stead and abolished their sacrifices, and the children of Israel remained without sacrifices and without altar, and without putting on the ephod and placing of incense; and He took away from them seers and prophets because they had not heard the great Prophet; and the former covenant was fulfilled by the latter, and the works which are in the law have grown old and become antiquated and fit for destruction, for from the time the new was given the old was abolished. And it was not only from the time of the advent of our Saviour that sacrifices were rejected, but even before (that) time their sacrifices did not give pleasure to Him, as it is written: "I will not eat the flesh of calves, and the blood of goats I will not drink"; but "sacrifice to God thanksgiving and accomplish thy vows to the Highest." And again He said: "A broken heart God does not reject." And again He said: "I have not desired sacrifices and by holocausts of peace (offerings) I have not been reconciled." "The sacrifices of God are an afflicted spirit." And also Isaiah the prophet said: "A multitude of your sacrifices I have not required, said the Lord." And again He said to them: "I hate and reject your feast days, and I will not smell in your sacrifices." |22

**7.** And this again is the word on which our Saviour says the law and the prophets depend, beautiful and good and seemly. For our Lord spake thus: "A single letter *yudh* shall not pass from the law or the prophets until all is done." For He took the law and the prophets and made them depend upon two commandments, and did not abolish anything from them. And when thou shalt look well at this word, so it truly is. The observation of that which is in the law and of everything which is written in it is an example of that word, "Thou shalt love the Lord thy God with all thy soul, and with all thy might, and with all thy heart"; and of everything which was done by the law, for it lead them to love the Lord their God; and a man shall love his neighbor as his own flesh. And these two commandments above are from the whole law. And when thou shalt set thy heart and look intently unto the law, in the beginning of all the law (thou shalt find) it is written thus: "I am the Lord thy God, who brought thee up from the land of Egypt. Thou shalt not make to thyself, My people, any image or any similitude." And the man who does not make another god has under him the word on which hangs the law and the prophets. Remember, beloved, that I have written for thee that the law is not imposed for the righteous, for he who observes righteousness is above the commandments and the law and the prophets; and the word which our Lord speaks is true: "The letter *yudh* shall not pass from the law and from the prophets," for by the two commandments He seals (them) and makes them depend.

**8.** Hear now, beloved, the persuasiveness of this word. If a man should say: "Why was this word written, that the seat of the children of Israel should remain in the land of Egypt four hundred and thirty years, when in the promise which had been made to Abraham it was said to him that there should be four hundred years? And thirty were received in addition?" Now I will show thee, beloved, even as it was. For when the time of fulfillment of the four hundred years was come, Moses was sent that he might deliver them. "When he killed the Egyptian, and they rejected him as their saviour, and Moses fled to Midian, wrath was upon them so that they remained thirty years in Egypt. For they said to Moses: "Who has appointed thee ruler and judge over us?" And when they rejected their salvation the wrath of God withheld them for thirty years in the midst of Egypt, and Moses was thirty years |23 in Midian. Then, when affliction increased upon them, He lead them out of Egypt. God manifested this patience of His spirit; first He chastised them because they had rejected Moses, and secondly because they had completed the sins of the Amorites. He exceeded that which had been promised to Abraham and added thirty years to the people, and He had patience with the Amorites seventy years, thirty in Egypt and forty in the desert. And when the four hundred and thirty was completed, and the forty years for the consummation of the iniquities of the Amorites, He brought them into the land of promise.

**9.** Know moreover, beloved, that there is no law for God. For sometimes He increases and diminishes, and sometimes He adds to because it is little. For in the days of Noah on account of the sins of men He promised that the days of men should be one hundred and twenty years, and in the six hundredth year of the years of the life of Noah He destroyed them. For He said: "A hundred and twenty years they shall be upon the earth." And in the six hundredth year of the years of the life of Noah they were destroyed, and he took away these twenty years. And again it is written that when iniquity increased the sins of the house of Ephraim, when Jeroboam ruled over them, the son of Nebat, that he sinned and caused Israel to sin, and when they sinned He promised in their behalf by the prophecy of Isaiah the prophet, who said to them that after sixty-five years He will cut off Ephraim from the people. This word was in the first year of Ahaz, and in the fourth year of Hezekiah Shalmanasar, King of Assyria ('Ôtûr), came up against them, and after him Taglathphalasar, and he carried them into exile from their land. For Ahaz reigned over them sixteen years, and in the fourth year of Hezekiah the kings of Assyria ruled over them; so there were only twenty years and He cut off Ephraim from the people of Israel, and He took away from them forty-five years, and this time which at first He had appointed He did not complete according to that which He had decreed.

**10.** It was not as though it were unknown that He had promised in their behalf that things should be thus, and then the years were diminished and also were increased, but as known; for He knew the measure of that which was to come, and on account of His mercies He gave a time for repentance that men might be without excuse; and men despised the longsuffering of God, and when they |24 heard that there was much time until the wrath which was promised should come, becoming bold they sinned before Him and said: "That which the prophets say is prophesied for a remote time." On account of this when there arose a disputing concerning these things in the days of Ezekiel the prophet and they said: "That which hath been prophesied is for a remote time," He said to Ezekiel: "As I live," saith the Lord of dominions, "there shall not again be a delay to My words, for the word which I shall speak I shall shortly accomplish." And He cut off that which He had foretold, to give to men a time for repentance, that perhaps they might repent; but they despised the longsuffering of God and did not repent, and He also changed the time which He had appointed and decreed to them. And it was not done as if it were not known, but as it is written: "Woe to him that destroyeth! Ye were not destroyed; and who hath spoken falsely, and He did not speak falsely against you. For when ye have wished to destroy ye have been destroyed, and when ye have wished to speak falsely it hath been spoken falsely against you." Again it is written in Jeremiah: "If I shall speak against a people and against a kingdom, to pluck up and to break down and to destroy them and to cause them to perish, and that nation shall turn from its wickedness, I also will make false My word, and I will turn away from them everything which I have spoken against them." Again Jeremiah said: "If I shall speak concerning a people and concerning a kingdom to build and to plant, and that people shall do iniquity before Me, I also will make false My word, and I will turn from it the good thing which I have spoken to benefit it."

**11.** Now, beloved, all these things have I written to thee because in what was said before, that is in the former discourse concerning faith, I have shown thee that in faith may be placed the foundation of this covenant in which we are established; and in this second discourse which I have written to thee I have reminded thee that all the law and the prophets depend upon two commandments, those which our Saviour spoke, and in these two commandments are included all the law and the prophets. And in the law faith is included, and by faith true love is established, which is from those two commandments, that after a man loves the Lord his God he shall cherish his neighbor as himself. |25

**12.** Now hear, beloved, concerning the love which is produced from those two commandments. For when our Life-giver came He showed the eagerness of love, for He said to His disciples: "This is My commandment that ye love one another." And again He said to them: "A new commandment I give you, that ye love one another." And again, when making clear concerning love, thus He warned them: "Love your enemies, and bless him who curses you; pray for those who deal hardly with you and persecute you." And this again He said to them: "If ye love him who loves you what is your reward? For if thou lovest him who loves thee thus also do the Gentiles, who loves them they love him." Again our Life-giver said: "If ye do good to him who does good unto you what is your reward? thus also do the publicans and sinners. But ye, because ye are called sons of God who is in heaven, be ye like Him who showeth mercy also upon those who renounce goodness." Again our Saviour said: "Forgive, and it shall be forgiven you; loose, and ye shall loosed; give, and it shall be given you." Again He spoke and put fear in us: "Unless ye forgive men who sin against you their sins, neither will the Father forgive you." For thus He warned and said: "If thy brother shall sin against thee, forgive him; and even if he shall sin against thee seven times in one day, forgive him."

**13.** And when Simon Peter (Kipho) heard this word he said to our Lord: "How many times, if my brother sin against me, shall I forgive him? Seven times?" Our Lord said to him: "Not only seven, but until seventy times seven (and) seven." Even if he shall sin against thee four hundred and ninety times, forgive him in one day" (this sentence has the particle indicating a quotation). And He is likened to His good Father who multiplied His forgiveness upon Jerusalem when He caused the children of Israel to go into captivity to Babylon, He scattered them seventy years, and when His mercies were revealed He brought them together to their land by means of Ezra the scribe, and He increased forgiveness unto them by the division of His day (which is) seventy weeks of years (cf. Ps. 90:4), four hundred and ninety years. And when they shed innocent blood He did not again exempt them on account of Jerusalem, but He delivered it over into the hands of its enemies, and they rooted it up, and they did not leave in it stone upon stone, and they did not leave its foundations for the |26 Lord. And He did not say to the children of Edom that vengeance should be recompensed them because they did not cry out against Jerusalem, "reveal it, reveal it, even to its foundations." But God by the division of His day forgave four hundred and ninety years, and He bore their iniquities; and then He rooted it up, and also He delivered Jerusalem into the hands of strangers. So our Life-giver commanded them that in one day a man should forgive his brother four hundred and ninety times.

**14.** But be not offended, beloved, by the word which is written unto thee, that by the division of His day God spared Jerusalem; for thus it is written by David in the ninetieth Psalms: "A thousand years in the eyes of the Lord are as a day which was completed and has passed away." And also our learned teachers say thus, that in the similitude of six days God made the world, and for the consummation of the world six thousand years were appointed, and there was to be a Sabbath of God in the similitude of the Sabbath which was after the six days, as our Saviour revealed and showed us concerning the Sabbath, for He spake thus: "Pray that your flight may not be in the Winter or on the Sabbath." And also the Apostle said: "There remaineth still a Sabbath of God. Let us give diligence also that we may enter into its rest."

**15.** Again when our Lord taught a prayer to His disciples, He said to them: "Thus shall ye pray, Forgive us our debts, and also we shall forgive our debtors." And again He said: "When thou desirest to offer an oblation, and thou rememberest that thou hast anger against thy brother, go away and be reconciled with thy brother, and then come (and) offer thy oblation." Lest when a man prayeth: "Forgive us our debts, and also we will forgive our debtors," he should be ensnared out of his own mouth, and it should be said to him by Him who receiveth prayers, thou thyself has not forgiven thy debtor, how shall it be forgiven to thee? And thy prayer shall remain upon the earth. And again our Lord shows us an example of that man who began to take a reckoning from his servants, and when his servant came into his presence who owed him ten thousand talents, and when his lord urged him that he give him what he owed him, and when he was unable to pay his debt to his lord, his lord commanded to release him and forgave him all that he owed. When that servant in his wickedness did not remember the forgiveness of his lord, how much he had |27 multiplied forgiveness towards him, and when he went forth he found one of his fellow-servants who owed him a hundred pence, and he held him, and choked him, and said to him, give me what thou owest me; and he did not receive the prayer which his fellow-servant asked from him, but going away he bound him in prison. And because he to whom much had been forgiven did not forgive his fellow-servant a little, he was given up to the officers who beat him until he gave what he owed. And He said to them: "Thus will My Father who is in heaven do to you if ye do not forgive each one his brother."

**16.** See again, beloved, how greatly the blessed Apostle magnified love when he said: "If ye are zealous of great gifts I will show you what is a more excellent gift." And he said: "If I have prophecy, and know all mysteries, and all knowledge, and all faith, so that I might remove a mountain, and love is not in me, I have gained nothing. And if I give all that I have to the poor to eat, and also deliver my body that it may be burnt, and love is not in me, again I have gained nothing." For he spake thus: "Love, its spirit is long-suffering and kind, and not envious, and also it is not boastful, and it is not puffed up, and does not seek anything which is pleasant for itself alone, but what is expedient for many. Love hopeth all things, suffereth all things, love is never cast down." Again he said: "Love is greater than all things." And the Apostle shows and demonstrates that after faith love excels, and on it a firm building has been established. And he shows prophecy to be built upon love, and mysteries to be made known by love, and knowledge to be fulfilled by love, and faith to be confirmed by love; and he who having faith moves a mountain, but has not love, profits nothing; and if a man give all that he has to the poor and his alms are not given in love, there is no advantage to him; and even if for the name of his Lord his body has been burnt in the fire, he has been in no wise profited. And again he shows that long-suffering, and patience, and kindness, and for a man not to envy his brother, these things are found in the fulness of love; and also patience, and humility and sweetness have been established in him by love. For faith has been erected upon the rock of a structure, and love is the bonds of the structure, and by it the walls of the house have been held together. And if a defect is found in the bonds of the house the whole structure | 28 will fall; so also when dissention is found in love all faith falls. And faith was not able to drive away jealousy and contention until the love of Christ came, just as a structure cannot be well built until the walls have been fastened by bonds.

**17.** Again I will show thee, beloved, that love is more excellent than anything else, and by it the righteous ones of the old times were perfected. For it (i. e. the

Scripture) shows concerning Moses that he gave himself in behalf of the sons of his people, and he wished that he might be blotted out of the book of life (if) only the people might not be blotted out. And also when they rose up against him to stone him, he offered up prayer before God in their behalf that they might be saved. And David also showed an example of love when he was persecuted by Saul, and a trap was continually set for his life so that they might kill him, and David by love was generously performing acts of mercies in behalf of Saul his enemy, who was seeking his life; and he was twice delivered into the hands of David, and he did not kill him and repaid good in place of evil. Because of this good did not depart from his house, and he who forsook him was forsaken. And Saul who repaid evil in place of good, evil did not depart from his house, and He called to God and He did not answer him, and he fell by the sword of the Philistines, and David wept over him bitterly. And David fulfilled beforehand the precept of our Saviour, who said: "Love your enemies," and "forgive, and it shall be forgiven unto you." Thus David loved and was loved, and forgave and it was forgiven unto him.

**18.** And Elisha also showed love in respect to this, when his enemies came against him to take him so that they might do evil to him, and he, doing good to them, set forth bread and water before them and sent them away from him in peace; and he fulfilled the word which is written: "If thine enemy is hungry feed him, and if he thirsts give him to drink." And also Jeremiah the prophet in behalf of those who made him a captive in a pit and were continually putting him to torture, but he also prayed ardently for them before God. And it was (by) this example of those who went before (that) our Saviour taught us that we should love our enemies and pray for those who hate us. And if He commanded us to love our enemies and to pray for those who hate us, what shall be our excuse to Him in the day of judgment, who have hated our brothers and |29 our own members? Because we are of the Body of Christ and members of His members. For he who hates one of the members of Christ will be separated from the whole body, and he who hates his brother will be separated from the sons of God.

**19.** And it was thus that our Saviour taught us diligently to manifest love. For first He perfected it in Himself, and then He taught those who heard Him. And He reconciled our enmity with His Father because He loved us, and He yielded up His innocence in the stead of the debtors, and the Good in place of the evil ones was put to shame, and the Rich in our behalf was made poor, and the Living died in behalf of the dead, and by His death made alive our death. And the Son of the Lord of all took for our sake the form of a servant, and He to whom all things were subject subjected Himself that He might release us from the subjection of sin. And by His great love He gave a blessing to the poor in spirit, and He promised the peace makers they should be called His brothers and sons of God; and He promised the humble that they should inherit the land of life; and He promised the mourners that by their supplications they would be comforted; and He promised to the hungry fulness in His kingdom; and to those who weep that they should rejoice in His promise; and He promised to the merciful that they should be shown mercy; and to these who are pure in heart He said that they should see God; and again He promised to those who are persecuted on account of righteousness that they should go into the kingdom of heaven; and to those who are persecuted on account of His Name He promised a blessing and rest in His kingdom. And He changed our nature of dust and made us the salt of truth, and He delivered us from being the prey of the serpent, and He called us the light of the world; and He delivered us from the power of death; and He made us good instead of evil, and pleasing instead of hateful; and He appointed for us mercy instead of hatred; and He imparted to us the perfect man; and He brought forth good things from His treasures, and delivered us from him who brought forth evil things from the superfluities of his heart.

**20.** And because of His overflowing love He healed the plagues of the sick; He healed also the son of the centurion because of his faith; and He silenced the waves of the sea by His power; and because of His favor He drove from us the evil spirits who were legion; and by His mercy He restored to life the daughter of the ruler of the |30 synagogue; and again He cleansed the woman from the pollution of blood; and He opened the eyes of two blind men who had come to Him; and also He gave to the Twelve power and authority over all disease and infirmity, and also to us by their hands. And He prohibited us from the way of the Gentiles and of the Samaritans. And He gave power to us by His mercy that we might not fear when they brought us before the rulers of the world. And He set a division in the earth because of His great peace. And He forgave the many sins to the woman who was a sinner because of His mercies. And He made us worthy because of His grace that we might build a tower at His expense (S. Lk. XIV: 28; here there appears to be a certain play upon words; tower, magdol, being suggested by the reference to S. Mary Magdalene in the preceding sentence). And He cast out from us unclean spirits, and He made us a lodging place of His divinity, and sowed in us a good seed which should give fruit a hundredfold, and sixtyfold and thirtyfold. And He was placed in the midst of the world in the likeness of a treasure which is put in a field. And He manifested the power of His greatness when He was cast down from on high to the depth and was not harmed. And He satisfied the hungry who had grown faint with five loaves and two fishes, five thousand men besides woman and children, and manifested the greatness of His glory. And on account of His abundant love He heard the Canaanitish woman and raised up her daughter from her infirmity. And by the power of Him who sent Him He loosed the tongue of the man who was dumb, and who was also deaf; and the blind saw His light, and by means of Him they glorified Him who had sent Him. And when He went up into the mountain to pray the rays of the sun were overcome by His light. And He made His power known in the case of that boy upon whom a spirit had come, and at His word the demon went away. And He gave us an example and a pattern that we should become as children and enter the kingdom of heaven. And He spoke and made clear concerning the little ones that a man should not despise them, that their angels always see the Father who is in heaven. And again He showed His healing perfectly in the case of that man who was infirm thirty-eight years, and He magnified His mercy towards him and healed him. And again He gave us a command, that weshould forsake the world and be turned to Him; and He revealed to us that he who is a lover of the world is not able |31 to be pleasing to God, by the example of the rich man who trusted in his goods; and by the case of that man who was made merry by his riches, and his destruction was in sheol, and he asked for water on the tip of his little finger, and no man gave to him. And He hired us as laborers that we should work in His vineyard, which is the vineyard of truth. All these things our Saviour did unto us because of His great love. And we also, beloved, should be partakers of the love of Christ, while we love one another and fulfil these two commandments, on which hang all the law and the prophets.

*The Demonstration Concerning Love Is Completed.*

# Demonstration VII: On the Penitents

(The following Homily, issued in 336-337 A.D., is especially valuable for its advanced teaching on the administration of penance and on pastoral care; there is nothing in either Greek or Latin Patristic literature of an equally early date which is quite so precise on either of these subjects).

**1.** Of all those who are begotten, who have put on a body, there is only One innocent, that is our Lord Jesus Christ; just as He bore witness concerning Himself, for He said: "I have overcome the world" (S. John 16: 33). And the prophet also bore witness con-cerning Him: "He did not iniquity, neither was guile found in His mouth" (Mal. 2: 6). And the blessed Apostle said: "He who had not known sin made Himself sin in our behalf" (2 Cor. 5; 21). And how did He make Himself sin? if not because of His taking sin, when He Himself had not committed it, and His nailing it on His cross. Again the Apostle said: "There are many who run in the race course, but one received the crown (1 Cor. 9: 24). Furthermore, there is no other of the sons of Adam who, descending into the contest, has not been smitten and beaten; for sin has reigned from (the time) that Adam transgressed against the commandment; and from the many it (sin) had beaten, and the many it had smitten, and the many it had killed, there was not a man from the many (that) it had not destroyed, until our Saviour came, and took it, and nailed it on His cross. And even when it was nailed on the cross there was (still) its sting, and it will sting many until the end, and (then) its sting will be broken.

**2.** For all diseases there are medicines, and there will be healing when a skilled physician shall have found them. And for those who have been smitten in our conflict there is the medicine of penitence, and those who apply it to their wounds are healed. O physicians! disciples of our wise Physician, take to yourselves this remedy, that |44 by it ye may heal the wounds of the sick. For warriors who are smitten in battle at the hands of one who is fighting with them, when they have found for themselves a skillful physician, give themselves over to him for their healing, that he may make whole the parts where they have been wounded. And when a physician heals him who has been smitten in battle, he receives gifts and honor from the king. So, beloved, he who is laboring in our conflict, and his enemy comes against him and smites him, it is fitting to give to him the medicine of penitence, when the repentance of him who has been smitten has become great. For God does not reject the penitent, for Ezekiel the prophet said: "I take no delight in the death which the sinner dieth, but that he may turn from his evil way and live" (33:11).

**3.** For he who is wounded in battle is not ashamed to give himself into the hands of a skillful physician in order that he may overcome that which befell him (in) battle; and the king does not reject him who has been healed, but numbers and considers him with his army. So the man whom Satan has smitten ought not to be ashamed to confess his sin, and depart from it, and entreat for himself the medicine of penitence. For gangrene comes to the wound of him who is ashamed to show it, and harm comes to his whole body; and he who is not ashamed has his wound healed, and again returns to go down into the conflict. And he who becomes gangrenous is not able to be healed, and may not put on again the arms which he laid aside. So for him who has been conquered in our conflict there is this way that he may be healed, when he shall say "I have sinned", and shall entreat penitence. And he who is ashamed is not able to be healed, because he does not wish to make known to the physician who receives two pennies (perhaps an allusion to S. Luke 10:35) his wounds, that by his means all the places where he has been smitten may be healed.

**4.** And to you physicians also, disciples of our illustrious Physician, it is fitting that you should not withhold healing from him who needs healing. Whosoever shows his wound to you, give to him the medicine of penitence; and whosoever is ashamed to show his disease, ye shall exhort him not to conceal from you, and when he has revealed to you do not publish it, lest by means of it the innocent also should be considered as debtors by enemies and those who hate (them). The line of battle where the slain are falling is considered by their enemies the weakest of them all. And when those who are |45 smitten are found among them, those who have not been smitten bind up their wounds, and there is no revealing of their condition to the enemy. But if it is made known to everyone about them the whole army bears a bad name; and also the king, the leader of the army, is angry with those who exposed his army, and they are smitten with wounds which are worse than those of the ones who were smitten in battle.

**5.** But if those who have been smitten are not willing to show their wounds the physicians are not liable to any blame, because they did not heal the infirm who have been smitten. And if those who have been smitten are desiring to hide their wounds, they will not again be able to wear arms on account of the gangrene contracted in their bodies. And while there is gangrene in them, and they attempt to wear arms, when they are going down to engage in conflict, their arms will become hot upon them, and their wounds will become corrupt and putrified, and they will be killed. And when the corpses of those who have hidden from them their wounds are found, then all the shame of those who have concealed the wounds of their smiting is laughed at; and their corpses also will not be committed to a grave, and they will be regarded as fools, and evil, and ignorant.

**6.** And also the one who showing his wound has been healed is careful of the place which has been healed that he may not be struck in it a second time. For the healing of him who has been smitten a second time will be difficult for a skilled physician, for the wound which is in the scar will not have been healed completely; and also, although it may be healed again, he will not be able to wear arms, and when he shall venture to wear arms he will be taking to himself a kind of condemnation.

**7.** O you who have put on the arms of Christ! learn the arts of war, lest ye be conquered and thrown down in the battle. Our enemy is cunning and skillful, but his arms are weaker than ours. Therefore it is right for us to engage (in battle) with him, and to take away his arms, being vigilant in sleep; for he is not visible to us when he is fighting with us. We turn unto Him who sees him, that He may take him away from us.

**8.** Also I counsel you who have been smitten that ye be not ashamed to say : "We have fallen in the battle." Receive the medicine which is without price, and repent, and live, before ye are slain. Also I remind you physicians of that which is written in the |46 Scriptures of our wise Physician, that He does not forbid repentance. For when Adam had sinned He called him to repentance when He said to him: "Adam, where art thou?" (Gen. 3: 8). And he, hiding his sin from Him who beholds the heart, laid the blame upon Eve who had deceived him. And because he did not confess his sin death was decreed against him and against all his offspring. And Cain also was full of guile, and sacrifice was not accepted from him; and He gave to him (a place) of repentance, and he did not accept. For He said to him: "if thou hadst done well I would have accepted thy sacrifice; but thou hast not done well and thy sin will accompany thee" (Gen. 4: 7). And in the guile of his heart he slew his brother and was accursed, "and he was trembling and wandering on the earth" (Gen. 4: 12). And also to the generation in the days of Noah he gave one hundred and twenty years for repentance; and they were not willing to repent and, one hundred years being completed, He destroyed them.

**9.** See also, beloved, how much better this is when a man confesses and turns away from his iniquity. Our God does not reject the penitent. For the Ninevites increased their sins, and they received the preaching of Jonah when he declared an overthrow against them, and they repented, and God was moved with compassion towards them. And the sons of Israel also when they increased their sins, and He proclaimed repentance to them, and they did not receive it; for He called to them by Jeremiah and said: "Repent, (become) penitent sons, and I will heal your penitence." Again He proclaimed in the ears of Jerusalem and said: "Return unto Me, a penitent daughter". Again He said unto the sons of Israel: "Return and be restored from your evil ways, and from the wickedness of your works." And thus He said to the people: "If thou return unto Me, I will restore thee, and thou shalt stand before Me." And again He spoke thus and reproached them: "I have said, Return unto Me, inhabitant (fem.) of Israel with all thy heart, and she has not returned" (these are all loose quotations from Jere. 3 and 4:1). Again He took up a parable against them and reminded them of that which is written in the law, and He wished that the law might speak falsely for the sake of their repentance. For He said: "When a man takes a wife and she shall go forth from him and shall be unto another man, and if the other man who took her shall die or shall dismiss her, and she shall return unto her first husband, it will not be possible for her first husband to |47 take her again after she has been polluted; and if he shall take her, behold that land will surely be polluted. And now also I have taken thee, Jerusalem, to Myself, and thou hast become Mine, and thou hast gone from Me, and thou hast departed, and thou hast committed fornication with stones and trees. Now return unto Me, and I will receive thee, and in thy repentance I will loose the law" (Jere. 3: 1 sqq., and Dt. 24: 13 sqq., both loosely).

**10.** Be ye not afraid, O penitents, lest the hope which is written in the Scriptures be cut off; for it is fitting for the Spirit of God thus to warn, for a fearful warning is set in Ezekiel the prophet when He said to him: "If all his days a man shall do judgment and righteousness, and at the end of his days he shall do iniquity, in his iniquity he shall die. And if a man shall do iniquity all his days, and he shall repent and do judgment and righteousness, his soul shall live" (Ezek. 33: 18-19). By this one word He has warned the righteous that he should not sin and lose his course; and He gave hope to the wicked that he should turn from his iniquity and live. Again He said to Ezekiel: "Although I cut off the hope of the unrighteous, thou shalt surely warn him; also when I encourage the righteous, set thou fear before him that he may be warned" (abridged thought of Ezek. 33: 7-9). When I say to the sinner: "Thou shalt surely die; and thou dost not warn him, the sinner shall die in his iniquity, and is blood will I require from thy hand" (Ezek. 3: 18), because thou didst not warn him. "And if thou warn the sinner, the sinner shall live whom thou shalt warn, and thou shalt save thy soul. And when thou shalt say to the righteous: thou shalt surely live, and there shall be confidence to him concerning this, it was fitting for thee to warn him lest he be exalted and sin; and he who has been warned shall live, and thou shalt save thy soul" (Ezek. 3: 17-21 loosely). Give heed again, penitents, to the hand which is stretched forth and the calling to repentance, for He spoke also by Jeremiah the prophet and gave repentance. For thus He said: "If I shall speak concerning a nation, and concerning a kingdom, to pluck up and to break down and to destroy and to cause it to perish; and that nation turn from its iniquity, I will turn away from it the evil which I had decreed against it. And if I shall speak concerning a nation and concerning a kingdom, to plant and to build, and there shall be confidence in it concerning this, and it do that which is evil in My sight, I also will turn from it the good which I had promised concerning it" (Jere. 18: 7-10), and in its iniquity and in its sins I will cause it to perish. |48

**11.** Hear again also ye who hold the keys of the gates of heaven and open the gates to the penitent, believe that which the blessed Apostle hath said: "If a man from among you shall be troubled by sin, ye who are in the spirit, restore ye him in a spirit of gentleness; and be ye cautious lost perhaps ye also be tempted" (Gal. 6: 1). For the Apostle was afraid and warned them, for he said concerning himself: "Lest I who have preached to others should myself become reprobate" (r Cor. 9: 27). He who from among you is troubled by sin, do not hold him as an enemy, but be ye counsellors and admonishers to him as of a brother; for he whom ye have separated from among you has been swallowed up by Satan. Again he said: "We who are strong ought to bear the infirmities of the weak (Rom. 15: 1). Again he said: "He who is lame should not be cast down, but should be healed" (Heb. 12: 13).

**12.** I say to you also, penitents, that ye should not withhold from your souls this counsel which is given for yourhealing. For he has said in the Scriptures: "He who confesseth his sins and passeth away from them, God will be moved with compassion in his behalf" (Prov. 28: 13). Behold the son who has squandered his goods, and when he returned unto his father he rejoiced over him, and received him, and killed for him the fatted ox, and his father was glad over his return. And he called his friends also that they might rejoice with him; and his father embraced him and covered him with kisses and said: "this my son was dead and is alive; he was lost and has been found (S. Luke 15: 32). And his father did not find fault with him about the goods which he had squandered.

**13.** And our Lord encouraged the penitents and said: "I have not come to call the righteous but sinners to repentance" (S. Luke 5:32). And again He said: "There shall be joy in heaven over onesinner that repenteth, more than over ninety and nine righteous persons, who are not needing repentance " (S. Luke 15:7). The shepherd in concerned about that sheep who is lost from all the flock more than (about) those who have not wandered. For Christ died because of sinners, not because of the righteous, as He said by the prophet: "He bore the sins of many" (Isa. 53:12). And the Apostle said: "If while we were sinners God was reconciled with us by the death of His Son, how much more abundantly now in His reconciliation shall we live by His life" (Rom. 5:10).

**14.** God forgives him who confesses his sins. For when David |49 had sinned, Nathan the prophet came unto him and made known to him his sin and the punishment which he should receive. Then David confessed and said: "I have sinned." The prophet said to him: "The Lord also hath put away thy sin because thou last confessed" (2 Sam. 12: 13). And when he prayed he spoke thus: "Against thee only have I sinned, and done evil things before Thee" (Ps. 51: 4). And again he entreated God and said: "Lead not Thy servant into judgment, for in Thy sight no man living is justified" (Ps. 143: 2). And Solomon also spake thus: "Who can say, Thou hast made my heart clean, and I have been cleansed from sins" (Prov. 20: 9)? And also in the law it is written that Moses prayed before God and said: "Thou forgivest iniquity and sin, and surely Thou dost not justify" (Ex. 34:7; Num. 14:18 loosely). And also when he wished that his people might be blotted out on account of their sins Moses spoke thus, when he entreated and supplicated and said: "Forgive Thy people its transgression, as Thou hast forgiven them from Egypt and up to to-day". And God said to him: "I forgive them according to Thy word" (Num. 14:19-20).

**15.** O ye who are entreating penitence, be ye like unto Aaron the chief of the priests who, when he had caused the people to sin by the calf, confessed about his sin and his Lord forgave him. And also David, the chief of the kings of Israel, confessed about his transgression, and it was forgiven him. And also Simon, the chief of the disciples, when he denied, (saying) that Christ hath never seen me, and he cursed and swore, "I do not know Him" (S. Mt. 26: 74) and when repentance came to him he multiplied tears in his weeping; our Lord received him, and made him the foundation, and called him Peter, the edification of the Church.

**16.** Be ye not foolish as Adam who was ashamed to confess his sin. And also be ye not likened to Cain who, when he was accused of killing his brother, said: "I do not know where Abel is, for I am not his keeper" (Gen. 4: 9). And be ye not lifted up on high in the mind in the likeness of the corrupt generation, and do not add iniquity to iniquity and increase your sins, thinking yourselves to be innocent while ye are debtors. Hearken to your first fathers who, even when they were righteous, subjected themselves to humiliation. For Abraham said: "I am dust and ashes" (Gen 18:27), and he held himself lowly as a thing of small consequence. And also David said: "The days of men are as a vapor" (Ps. 144: 4). And | 50 Solomon spoke and admonished: "If the righteous shall scarcely be saved where shall the sinners and the impious be found" (Prov. 11:31; cf. 1 S.Peter 4: 18)?

**17.** I beseech thee, beloved by the mercies of God, not on account of that which I have written unto thee of God who does not reject the penitent, that thou do not let go thy fortitude and become lacking in repentance. To the needy only is repentance given. Therefore let this be (a care) to thee that there may not be need for repentance. This hand is stretched forth to sinners, and the righteous do not seek it. For alms are given to the poor, and the rich have no need for them. They give to the man who has been stripped by robbers, who is ashamed, that he may be clothed, that he may cover his shame. Do not lose that which thou be wearied in seeking it again, or (uncertain) whether thou canst find it again or not. And even when thou hast found much it is not like thy own possession; for he who has sinned and repented is not equal to him who has kept himself far from sin. Thou shouldest be loving the higher part and keeping far from that which is inferior; by thine arms the good should be fought for, lest thou be smitten in the battle, that thou mayest not have need for seeking a remedy, and be wearied in going the way to the house of the physician. And when thou art perfectly healed these scars will be recognized. Do not be confident that there will be healing for thee, and give thyself the name of one who is humble, but be greater by means of repentance. He who has torn his garment needs (a patch) upon it that it may be filled up, and even though it has been well sewn everyone discerns it. And he who breaks down a hedge built for him by toil, even though it be well (re-) built, it is called broken. And he whose house thieves break though, it has been laid open from within and the hole is recognized, and by great toil some of that which was lost may be regained. And he who cuts down his fruit tree, it will be a long time until it grows up again (lit. changes) and gives fruit. And he who opens up his drinking fountain, labors and toils until he closes it, and when it is well closed he fears lest, perhaps, the waters increasing, it should ruined. And he who gathers the flower of his vineyard at its season is deprived of the fruit of grapes. And there are blushes on the face of him who steals, and he toils and labors until the penalty his remitted to him. And he who throws down his work in a vineyard receives (his) pay and, his head bowed down, is unable to ask for more. And he who subdues the power |51 of his youth will rejoice in his old age. And he who does not drink of stolen waters will be refreshed at the fountain of life (N. B. The argument of this section is far from clear).

**18.** O ye who have been called to the conflict, hear the sound of the trumpet and be of good cheer. And also I speak to you, bearers of the trumpets, priests, doctors and wise men, assemble and say to all the people: "He who fears let him turn away from the conflict, lest he break the heart of his brethren, even as his heart (is broken). And he who has planted a vineyard let him return to his husbandry, lest being anxious about it he fail in the battle. And he who has married a wife and wishes to take her, let him return and rejoice with his wife. And he who has built a house let him return to it, lest perhaps he be mindful of his house and does not fight perfectly". Conflict is seemly only for those that, setting their faces to (those things which are) before them, are not mindful of anything which is behind them. For their treasures are before them, and all that which they plunder is their own, and they receive their profit from that which they win. Therefore, I speak to you, sounders of the trumpets, when ye have finished admonishing look to those who are turning back, and care for those who are remaining, and lead down to the waters of probation those who are assembling themselves for battle. Everyone who is strong the waters will prove, and those who are slothful will be separated thenceforth.

**19.** Hear then, beloved, this mystery which Gideon foresaw and showed figuratively. When he assembled the people for battle, the scribes, the fulfillers of the law, he admonished (according to) the words which I have written above unto thee; then many people with drew from the army, and when those who were left were chosen for battle, "the Lord said to Gideon, lead them down to the water and there prove them. He who laps up the water with his tongue (Jud. 7: 5) is eager and courageous to go forth to battle; "and he who falls down upon his belly to drink the water" is faint (hearted) and afraid to go forth to battle. Great, then, is this mystery, beloved, which Gideon foresaw, and it shows a type of baptism, and the mystery of the conflict, and an example of anchorites. For he foresaw and warned the people from the first by the probation of the water. Also when he tried them by the water from the ten thousand only three hundred men were chosen to wage war. This also agrees with the word of our Lord, who said: "many are called, few are chosen" (S. Mt. 22: 14). |52

**20.** For this reason it is fitting for the sounders of trumpets, the preachers of the Church, to warn all (who are in) the covenant of God [1] before baptism, and to those who choose for themselves virginity and holiness, young men and virgins and those (wishing to. become) holy; and for the preachers to warn them and say: "He who sets his heart upon the natural state of fellowship (*i.e.* in matrimony), let him become united before baptism lest, perhaps, he fall in the conflict and be killed. And he who is afraid of this part of the struggle let him turn back lest, perhaps, he break the heart of his brethren as well as his own heart. And he who loves possessions let him turn back from the army lest, perhaps, when the battle shall prevail against him he should remember his possessions and turn back to them, for there is disgrace to him who turns back from the conflict". And he who does not offer himself, and does not yet put on arms, is not blamed if he turns back; but everyone who has offered himself and put on arms is derided if he turns back from the conflict. It is fitting to him to empty himself for the strife, for he may not be mindful of anything which is behind and turn back to it.

**21.** And when they have preached and delivered their message and warned all (who are in) the covenant of God, they will bring to the waters of baptism those who have been chosen for the conflict and have been tried. And after baptism they will take heed to those who are strong and to those who are weak; it is fitting to encourage the strong and, furthermore, they should openly turn back from the conflict those who are faint (hearted) and weak, lest when hardship approach them they should hide their arms and flee and be overcome. For He said to Gideon: "Lead down to the water" those who present themselves. And when he had brought the people down to the water "the Lord said to Gideon, all those who lap the water as a dog laps with his tongue" shall go with thee to battle. "And all those who throw themselves down to drink water shall not go with thee to battle." Great is this mystery, beloved, which he provided and showed (as) His sign to Gideon. For He said to him: "Everyone who laps the water as a dog laps is fit to go to battle." And from every living creature which has been created there is not one which loves his master and keeps watch over him by day and by night as does a dog, | 53 and even when his master beats him severely he does not depart from him, and when he goes forth to the hunt with his master and a powerful lion meets his master he delivers himself over to death instead or his master. So are those strong who have been put to the test by the water; they follow their Master as the dogs, and they delivert themselves over to death for Him, and carry on His struggle valiant ly, and keep watch over Him by day and by night, and they roar like the dogs while they meditate upon the law day and night (cf. Heb. Ps. 1: 2), and they love the Lord, and they lick His wounds when they receive His Body, and they set Him before their eyes, and they lick Him with their tongues as a dog licks his master. And those who do not meditate upon the law are called "dumb dogs, who are not able to bark" (Isa. 56: 10); and all those who are not eager to last are called "greedy dogs, not knowing how to be satisfied" (Isa. 56:11). And those who are eager to seek mercies receive the bread of children, and they cast it to them (cf. S. Mt. 15: 26).

**22.** And again the Lord said to Gideon: "Those who fall down to drink water shall not go with thee to battle, lest they fall down and be conquered in battle." For those who falling down drank the water slothfully foreshowed a mystery. Wherefore, beloved, it is necessary for the ones who fall in the conflict not to be made like to these slothful ones, lest they turn back from the struggle and become a reproach to all their comrades.

**23.** Hear also, beloved this word lest, since I have persuaded thee from the Scriptures that God does not reject penitents, thou trust to thyself and venture to sin; and lest on account of what I have spoken to thee (any one) become remiss and be smitten (because) he does not seek repentance. For thus it is fitting for him to remain in sadness all his days, lest he become proud and condemnation be upon him. The servant who offends against his master changes his garment that his master may be reconciled to him, comes before (him), and makes himself obscure in his presence, that perhaps he may receive him. And when his master perceives that he is faithful to him, he forgives him his offence and is reconciled to him. For if he say to his master, "I have offended against thee," his master would show mercy to him; but if when he has offended he should say to his master, "I have not sinned, "he would add to the anger of his master against him. Remember, beloved, the son who squandered his goods, and when he confessed to his father he forgave him his wrongdoings. And also the |54 woman who had multiplied wrongdoings, when she came to the Lord He forgave her many sins and had mercy upon her. And Zacchaeus the publican was also a sinner, and he confessed his sins and the Lord forgave him. And also our Saviour spoke thus: "I came not to call the righteous, but sinners to repentance" (S. Lk. 5: 32). For the Lord died for sinners, and His comming was not in vain. And also the Apostle said about himself: "I was a blasphemer, and a persecutor, and a reviler (1 S. Tim. 1: 13), and God had mercy upon me. Again he spoke thus: "Christ died in our behalf" (1 Thess. 5: 9-10). For from the whole flock its Lord seeks the sheep which is lost, and finds it, and rejoices over it. And there is joy to the watchers of heaven when a sinner turns back from his iniquity. "For it is not the will of the Father who is in heaven that one of these little ones should perish" (S. Mt. 18: 14), who have sinned and who have sought repentance for themselves. "For the Lord came not that He might call the righteous but sinners to repentance." Whosoever is sick among you we bear his sufferings, and whosoever offends we are afflicted in his behalf.

**24.** For when sickness comes to one of our members we occupy ourselves with his wound until he is made whole; and when one of our members is glorified the whole body shines and is beautiful; and when sickness comes to one of our members fever burdens the whole body. "Every one who shall cause one of these little ones to offend shall fall into the sea with the mill stone of an ass on his neck" (S. Mt. 18: 6). And he who rejoices over the evil of his brother shall soon be crushed himself. And he who treads with his foot upon his brother shall not be spared. For the wound of the scoffer there is no healing, and the sins of the mockers shall not be forgiven. For he who digs a pit shall fall into it; and he who rolls away a stone it shall return upon him. And he who stumbles and falls let him not say, every man is like me; and let not the rich man who draws near to poverty say, all the rich are like unto me, for if his prayer is heard who is there that will supply his loss?

**25.** All these things I have written unto thee, beloved, because in our age there are those who themselves choose to become solitaries, sons of a covenant, and religious. And we have engaged in conflict against our adversary, and our adversary is fighting against us that he may lead us back to the nature from which in our freedom we have separated ourselves. And there are some of us who are vanquished |55 and swallowed up, and when those who are vanquished justify themselves and, even though we know their sins, confirm themselves in that thought and do not wish to draw near to repentance, they, on account of their shame, die the second death, and are not mindful of Him who searches the consciences. And again there is one who confesses his sin, and penitence is not given to him. O master of the house of Christ, give penitence to thy fellow man, and remember that the Lord did not reject the penitent. Tares are sown in the field, and the Master of the seed does not permit His servants to purge the tares from among the wheat until the time of harvest. A net is spread in the sea, and the fish are not chosen until it is drawn to the top. Servants receive hire from their masters, and his master will judge the slothful servant. The wheat and the chaff are mingled together, and the Lord of the threshing-floor separates and cleanses (them). There are many who are called to the marriage feast, and His Lord casts out him who has not garments into the darkness. The wise and the foolish are standing together, and the Lord of the bride-chamber knows who shall enter.

**26.** O shepherds, disciples of the Lord, feed the flock and lead (it) well! Strengthen the sick, support the weak, bind up the broken, make whole the lame, and take heed to the fattened ones for the Lord of the flock. Be not likened unto an unskilled and foolish shepherd, who in his foolishness is not able to feed the flock, and whose arm is dried up, and whose eye has been blinded, because he said: "dying, let it die; and perishing, let it perish, and the flesh that is left shall be eaten by its companions ". And when the Chief of the shepherds comes He will condemn the unskilled and foolish shepherd who has not cared well for his fellow servants. And he who has shepherded the flock and led (it) well shall be called "a good and skillful servant" (cf. S. Mt. 25: 21), who has presented the flock to the Shepherd while it was intact. O watchers, watch well, and admonish all the people concerning the sword, lest it come and take away the soul. For that soul is taken away in its sins, and its blood will be required from your hands. But if the soul is taken away after admonition, that soul will be taken away in its own sins, and ye will not be trodden down. O fattened flock, do not smite the weak, lest ye be condemned in judgment by our great Shepherd when He shall come.

**27.** Receive this exhortation, beloved, which conducts the penitents and admonishes the righteous. This is a world of grace, and |56 until it is finished there is repentance in it. The time approaches in which grace vanishes and justice reigns; and in that time there is no repentance and justice rests tranquilly, because grace in its strength has prevailed. And when the time of justice approaches grace is unwilling to receive penitents, because a limit is set (at) the departure (from this life), thenceforth there is not again repentance. Read, beloved, and learn, and know, and perceive, for in regard to this every man is needing in part; for there are many who are running in the race course, and the victor receives for himself the crown, and every man according to his labor shall receive his reward.

*The demonstration concerning penitents is completed*

Made in the USA
San Bernardino, CA
02 April 2016